Ideas of the Modern World

Fundamentalism

Alex Woolf

D1385087

Raintree

Chicago, Illinois

Customer Service 888-363-4266
Visit our website at www.raintreelibrary.com

Copyright Permissions
Raintree
100 N. LaSalle
Suite 1200
Chicago, IL 60602

Library of Congress Cataloging-in-Publication Data:

Woolf, Alex.
  Fundamentalism / Alex Woolf.
    v. cm. -- (Ideas of the modern world)
  Includes bibliographical references and index.
  Contents: What is fundamentalism? -- Christian fundamentalism -- Islamic fundamentalism -- Other forms of fundamentalism -- Comparing fundamentalisms -- The future of fundamentalism.
  ISBN 0-7398-6416-5 (hardcover)
  1. Fundamentalism--Juvenile literature. [1. Fundamentalism. 2.
Religions. 3. Religion and society.] I. Title. II. Series.
  BL238.W66 2003
  200'.9'04--dc21

2003000912

1 2 3 4 5 6 7 8 9 0
LB 08 07 06 05 04

Acknowledgments
The publisher would like to thank the following for permission to reproduce photographs:

pp. 4, 24, 38, 41, 42, 48, 49, 51, 52, 53, 58, 59 Popperfoto/Reuters;
p. 6 Popperfoto(Reuters/Popperfoto/Jorge Silva); pp. 7, 10, 12, 18, 21, 25, 56-57 Corbis;
p. 8 The Bridgeman Art Library (Archives Charmet); p. 9 Topham Picturepoint (Topham/Photri); pp. 13, 20 and title page Topham Picturepoint (Tony Savino/The ImageWorks) pp. 15, 17, 26–27, 31, 36, 43, 47 Popperfoto; p. 22, 23, 37 SIPA/Rex;
p. 29 The Bridgeman Art Library (Index);
p. 30, 35 Topham Picturepoint (Topham/Associated Press); p.32 Peter Sanders; p. 44 Rex (ACT); p. 45 Topham Picturepoint (Topham/Associated Press);
p. 46 Topham Picturepoint (Topham/The ImageWorks); p. 50 Chapel Studios;
p. 55 Topham Picturepoint (Topham/Associated Press).

Cover photo shows an open Bible © Royalty-Free/CORBIS

Series design: Simon Borrough

Printed in Hong Kong

Contents

What Is Fundamentalism?

In its strictest sense, fundamentalism means a belief in the **literal** truth of a sacred text. Put another way, fundamentalists believe that the words of the holy book of their religion are the exact truth and are not open to different interpretations. In everyday English the word "fundamentalist" is often used to describe someone who is very strict or **conservative** in his or her beliefs.

Fundamentalists are found in nearly all the world's major religions. They are people who care deeply about the traditions of their religion, and they strongly oppose attempts to reform their beliefs or adapt them to new ways of thinking. They believe that theirs is the only true religion, and are sometimes intolerant of the beliefs of others.

The term "fundamentalism" originated in the United States in the early part of the 20th century, and was used to describe a movement within the Protestant

In January 2002 women in Pakistan chant slogans, demanding the release of imprisoned Islamic fundamentalist leader, Qazi Hussein Ahmed.

The origin of the term

The term "fundamentalism" was invented in 1920 by an American journalist and preacher named Curtis Lee Laws. He used it to describe the **anti-modern movement** of American Protestants that had emerged since the end of the 1800s. Between 1910 and 1915, a leading group of Protestant churchmen had published a series of twelve pamphlets entitled *The Fundamentals of the Faith*, which inspired the term fundamentalism. These pamphlets claimed that there were several fundamentals of Church **doctrine** (principles forming the basis of a belief) that all Christians must believe in. These included the infallibility of the **Bible**, the sinfulness of humanity, the virgin birth of Jesus, and humankind's **salvation** through Jesus' death. Curtis Lee Laws described fundamentalists as those "who still cling to the great fundamentals and who mean to do battle royal" for the Christian faith.

Church. Since the 1980s the meaning of the term has been broadened to include religious movements of other faiths. Not all of these movements assert the literal truth of a sacred text, yet they share many of the other qualities of the original fundamentalists, and so have been described as fundamentalist.

In this book we will look at the phenomenon of fundamentalism, examining the similarities between the movements, the dynamics that cause them to arise, and their impact on society. We will also look at specific forms of fundamentalism—particularly Christian and Islamic—discussing their history, present-day significance, and possible future development.

The characteristics of fundamentalism

Fundamentalist movements from different religions—and even from within the same religion—vary greatly. Their particular nature is dependent on the traditions and culture of the religion and society from which they sprang. However, they do tend to have certain characteristics in common.

As has been said, most fundamentalists believe in what they interpret as the literal truth of their particular sacred text, whether it be the Christian **Bible**, the Muslim **Qur'an,** or the Jewish **Torah**. They consider every sentence of that text to be fact, and not a story or a myth. In their view, the text comes straight from God, is perfect, and is never wrong. Because of this fundamentalists often want laws and principles within that text enforced throughout society.

Fundamentalists are often strongly opposed to anything that contradicts their interpretation of God's laws, especially with regard to matters of human relationships and the family. Many of them oppose homosexuality, abortion, and the idea of equal status for women and men. They wish to impose their views on the rest of society.

It is common for fundamentalists to believe in an ideal time in the past—a golden age—when people

Jewish men reading the Torah. Orthodox Jews believe that the Torah is God's teaching to people, telling them how to live and behave. The Torah also contains stories about Jewish history and the Jews' relationship with God.

> Randall Terry, founder of Operation Rescue, a **militant** Christian fundamentalist group opposed to abortion, said on August 16, 1993:
>
> *"I want you to just let a wave of intolerance wash over you. I want you to let a wave of hatred wash over you. Yes, hate is good…. Our goal is a Christian nation. We have a Biblical duty, we are called by God, to conquer this country."*

lived according to God's laws. They see themselves at the forefront of the struggle to restore that golden age. For Protestants this perfect time existed during the period of the early Church, while for Muslims it occurred in Arabia in the 600s, during the lifetime of the prophet Muhammad.

The causes of fundamentalism

Fundamentalist movements often arise when a religion is perceived to be under threat. Fundamentalists belive that one of the main threats to religion today is that society in general has become more **secular** (not connected with a church or religion). The role of religion in society has changed from that of a central guiding principle of government and law to a matter of personal choice. This process, known as **secularism**, has occurred at different times and speeds around the world. It occurred in the Christian West in the 1700s and 1800s, and in the Muslim world in the 1800s and the 1900s.

Randall Terry delivering a sermon. Fundamentalist groups are often led by a charismatic individual— someone who articulates the group's desires and fears, and influences their thinking.

This medieval painting shows a story from the Bible in which Jesus fed 5,000 people with just five loaves of bread and two fishes. Some Christians believe that the miraculous tales in the Bible really happened, even though some defy scientific explanation.

One early Protestant fundamentalist preacher, John Roach Straton (1875–1929), pointed to the latest scientific knowledge as evidence for the existence of God:

"The whole great machine that we call the universe seems to move with a precision and accuracy that is staggering to the finite mind.... In the realm of physics and chemistry, the same unvarying system is discovered.... What does it all mean? It manifestly means, for one thing, that God has a mission and a designed place for every atom of matter and every ounce of physical force in the entire universe."

The dominance of Western culture in the world today means that most regions and religions have been affected by **secularism.** Some people, frustrated at how their community can lose touch with traditional religious principles, have formed fundamentalist movements as a way of opposing secularism.

The challenge of science

Secularism has led to other threats to religion—and causes of fundamentalism. For example, science, because it offers people an alternative way of looking at the world, presents a major challenge to religion. It teaches people about the natural causes of events, and offers choices in how to handle events. For example, when they are sick many people both pray for recovery and visit a doctor. Science also appears to disprove, or cast into doubt, parts of the "never-wrong" sacred texts. For example, scientific discoveries have shown that Earth is a lot older than the Christian Bible implies. **Evolution,** a theory first put forward in the 1800s, suggests that humans were not created in their present form—as in the story of Adam and Eve—but may have developed from earlier life forms.

Secularism can also lead to changes in society, including a transformation of the traditional roles played by men and women. In some countries, like the United States, some women now have the same education and career opportunities as men. They have more control over when to have babies. Some Christian fundamentalists, upholding traditional roles for women as wives and mothers, discourage women from pursuing careers. In other societies where women have fewer opportunities, fundamentalists fiercely oppose allowing women freedom and equality in the way they live their lives.

Under the fundamentalist Taliban regime of Afghanistan (1995-2001), women were not allowed to go out without wearing a burka, which covered every part of their bodies. Girls could not go to school, and women were not permitted to work.

Christian Fundamentalism

Christian fundamentalism is, for the most part, an American movement. Its roots can be traced to the mid-1700s. Between 1730 and 1779, the American colonies (which would later become the United States) experienced an upsurge of religious feeling known as the First Great Awakening. Preachers were at the forefront of the movement, delivering powerful and theatrical sermons intended to scare people into being good Christians by evoking frightening images of Hell. These preachers stressed the powerlessness of humans to achieve **salvation** without the intervention of God.

Born again

The First Great Awakening was followed, at the beginning of the 1800s, by a new movement called the Second Great Awakening.

Jonathan Edwards (1703–1758) was one of the most fiery preachers of the First Great Awakening. Here is an excerpt from one of his sermons:

"The God that holds you over the pit of hell, much as one holds a spider, or some loathsome insect over the fire, abhors [hates] you, and is dreadfully provoked... you are ten thousand times more abominable in his eyes, than the most hateful venomous serpent is in ours.... O sinner! Consider the fearful danger you are in: It is... a wide and bottomless pit, full of the fire of wrath, that you are held over in the hand of that God."

George Whitefield (1714–1770) was one of the most famous preachers of the First Great Awakening. It was said that his voice could be heard a mile away, and his open-air sermons attracted crowds of up to 100,000.

What is Christianity?

Christians are followers of Jesus of Nazareth, a Jewish preacher and healer who lived in the Roman province of Palestine around the first century C.E. Christians believe that Jesus is the Son of God, who chose to take human form to save people from sin and bring them back to God. After Jesus' death, his followers traveled far and wide and encouraged many to convert to the new religion. Accounts of his life and teachings, as well as the acts and writings of his early followers, make up the New Testament of the **Bible**.

There are many different traditions within Christianity, usually called Churches. These have arisen through disagreements about the teachings, and different ways of worshiping. In the 1000s, Christianity split into the Orthodox Church and the Catholic Church. By the 1500s, many in the Catholic Church believed it had become corrupt, and a new movement known as Protestantism broke away from it.

From the beginning Protestantism was never one movement, but was made up of several denominations (groups), including Lutherans, Anglicans, and Calvinists. Other Protestant denominations have been established since, including Methodists, Episcopalians, Baptists, Presbyterians, and Quakers.

Today Christianity is the largest of all the world's faiths, with a total membership of almost two billion. There have been attempts to bring the Christian traditions closer together, and some have reunited. However, new movements are also arising in many parts of the world.

This was a more optimistic movement, which suggested that humans could save themselves by their own moral actions, by renouncing sin, and through surrender to God. This was called being "born again."

The 1830s and 1840s witnessed the emergence of the American **millenarian movement**. The millenarians believed that every word of the Bible was true, and that, according to the Biblical Book of Revelation, the second coming of Jesus Christ would soon occur, to be followed by a thousand years of peace, known as "the millennium."

By the end of the 1800s, the Church was facing challenges on all sides. The rapid growth in the manufacturing industry, known as the **Industrial Revolution**, had led millions of people to move to the cities in search of jobs. Communities that had traditionally been based around local churches were broken up, and consequently Christianity began to lose its dominant place in people's lives. Education, health care, and welfare, which had previously been controlled by the Church, became the responsibility of governments. A rising tide of **immigrants** brought other religions, particularly Roman Catholicism, to America. These religions challenged Protestantism as the nation's dominant **creed**.

Faith came to be seen more as a matter of personal choice than as something to be enforced by governments and law courts. With churches no longer as influential in guiding people's thinking and behavior, social attitudes also changed. People began to challenge traditional views, for example, about the role of women. Many Protestants, fearful of the threats to their traditions, joined the **millenarian movement.** They were particularly disturbed by the new field of biblical criticism in which scholars studied the Bible as if it were any other ancient text, and not the authoritative word of God.

Harry Emerson Fosdick, a liberal Protestant minister, was a central figure in the fundamentalist debate of the 1920s. His anti-fundamentalist sermon "Shall the Fundamentalists Win?", delivered in 1922, caused an uproar and led to his resignation in 1925.

In 1902, some millenarians joined with others who believed in the **literal** truth of the Bible to form the American Bible League, with the aim of promoting the Bible as a sacred work immune to criticism. Millenarians also participated in writing twelve pamphlets entitled *The Fundamentals of the Faith,* which led to the coining of the "fundamentalism" as a term. In 1919, the millenarians changed their name to the World's Christian Fundamentals Association (WCFA) and, by 1921, they had become known simply as fundamentalists. The WCFA acted as an umbrella organization for fundamentalists from different Protestant groups. It lasted until the 1940s.

The evolution controversy

During the 1920s a major focus of the fundamentalist movement was the teaching of the **theory of evolution** in schools. This theory was first developed in the 1800s by the biologist Charles Darwin (1809–1882), who claimed that human beings, and other creatures, evolved from earlier animals through a process known as **natural selection**. According to this theory, humans are part of a family of animals known as primates, which includes apes, with whom we share a common ancestor.

This 1874 cartoon compares Charles Darwin to an ape. Many believed, wrongly, that Darwin had claimed humans were descended from apes.

Dwight Lyman Moody (1837–1899)

Moody, a leading figure in the millenarian movement, left his family's farm at the age of seventeen to go to work in Boston, Massachusetts. While there he converted to Evangelicalism, a form of Protestantism that stresses the authority of the Bible and salvation through personal acceptance of Jesus as savior. In 1860, having moved to Chicago, he gave up his business in order to do charitable work in the city slums. Moody was a powerful and intense speaker, whose sermons stressed a literal interpretation of the Bible and looked forward to the second coming of Christ. He hated the trend of biblical criticism and the theory of evolution.

The theory of evolution challenges the biblical view of human origin presented in the book of Genesis. Genesis tells that God created the first humans, Adam and Eve, in God's image. Many people at this time—not just fundamentalists—found it deeply distasteful to think that, far from being created in the likeness of God, humans were descended from ape-like creatures. The fundamentalists were therefore able to recruit many supporters to their cause.

Fundamentalists campaigned throughout the 1920s against the teaching of evolution. They pressured politicians in eleven states to introduce **legislation** forbidding any teaching that contradicted the biblical view of creation. They succeeded in one state—Tennessee. In 1925 a science teacher named John Scopes, from Dayton, Tennessee, was taken to court for teaching evolution. The fundamentalists won the case, but the reports of the trial in the newspapers ridiculed the fundamentalists' **literal** interpretation of the Bible.

A period of consolidation

During the 1930s and 1940s, the fundamentalists faded from the national spotlight, as they focused less on political campaigning and more on developing their institutions. Many fundamentalists broke away from their denominations to found new churches. They also established schools that teach

The Scopes trial

During the hot summer of 1925, the attention of the world was focused on the trial in a Tennessee courtroom of the high school teacher John T. Scopes. It promised to be a dramatic showdown between fundamentalist believers in the Biblical story of creation and supporters of Darwin's theory of evolution. The prosecution case was argued by the famous **Democrat** politician and fundamentalist, William Jennings Bryan. Trial lawyer Clarence Darrow led for the defense. Darrow repeatedly humiliated Bryan by forcing him to confront apparent contradictions in the supposedly literal truth of the Biblical text. However, the judge would not allow these arguments to stand, and limited the trial to the single question: did Scopes teach evolution? No one could argue that he didn't, and Scopes was found guilty and fined $100. The law banning the teaching of evolution in Tennessee was eventually repealed in 1967.

John Scopes, the biology teacher, charged with illegally teaching the theory of evolution, on his way into court with his defense lawyer, Clarence Darrow (wearing a hat).

courses only in the Bible, and colleges. These would form the foundation of modern Christian fundamentalism. As well as teaching students, many of these schools also published magazines, hosted conferences, and started their own radio stations.

To keep themselves separate from the corrupting influences of secular America, fundamentalists created a whole set of institutions that paralleled the professional and business organizations of society. Students, teachers, doctors, scientists, social workers, and businesspeople with fundamentalist views could all join groups that specialized in their particular interest or occupation.

Communism

During the 1950s fundamentalism reemerged as a political force, mainly because of the growing fear of Communism that overtook the United States at that time. Communism is a political movement that stands in opposition to capitalism (the economic system that operates in the United States). Communist revolutionaries had taken power in Russia in 1917, renaming it the Soviet Union. By the late 1940s, the Soviet Union had grown to rival the United States in terms of military power, and Communism had attracted many supporters in Europe and, to a lesser extent, in the United States. Many Americans feared the spread of Communism and the threat they believed it posed to their way of life.

For fundamentalists the most worrying aspect of Communism was its rejection of God and religion. Communists saw Christianity and other faiths simply as a way of keeping the working classes in their place. Karl Marx, an early Communist thinker, called religion "the opium of the people." For this reason above all, fundamentalists regarded Communism as an evil that it was their duty to oppose.

It is certainly true that Communists saw many of the institutions of Western society, such as the family and religion, as part of the **exploitative** system they wished to replace. However, Communism was never as strong in the United States as those who opposed it claimed. Anti-Communism was used more as a convenient way of rallying people to the cause of fundamentalism.

The Evangelicals

During the 1950s fundamentalists were divided on how best to carry forward their message. Some wished to remain separate from modern society, which they saw as sinful and beyond salvation, and to live and

Right: Billy Graham preaching in 1954. Graham's crusades have taken him to Europe, Africa, Russia, and the Far East. He is said to have preached about Christianity to more people than any other person in history.

work within the alternative institutions they had created. Others believed that it was important to mix with the world, while remaining true to their fundamental Christian beliefs.

This second group called themselves Evangelicals (a revival of an old 19th century movement). Like the preachers of the Second Great Awakening, Evangelicals believed that anyone could find salvation by leading a moral life. By praying and reading the **Bible,** by not smoking or drinking alcohol, and through a **baptism** that they called being "born again" all could be "saved."

William Franklin Graham (1918–)

The Evangelicals found a champion in a young Baptist evangelist named Billy Graham. His popularity with the wider public and his great skills as a speaker helped to get the Evangelical movement noticed and made its arguments more convincing. Graham went on long preaching tours, known as crusades, and regularly appeared on radio and, later, television. As his fame spread, he became friendly with several U.S. presidents, but he always avoided speaking on political issues. This politically "neutral" stance helped to widen his appeal.

The 1960s was a decade of material wealth, but also of increasing consciousness about social inequalities. It was a time of student protests, the antiwar movement, and campaigns for women's rights. The Evangelicals were outspoken in their opposition to these trends. They campaigned against the newly available contraceptive pill, the notion of gender equality, and the toleration of homosexuality.

Followers of preacher and broadcaster Carl McIntire

Unlike the fundamentalists, the Evangelicals were happy to work with non-Protestant **conservatives** in their campaigns. For this reason they did not always use religious language to justify their position, but characterized it as a general concern for the erosion of "family values." Their strong stand brought them much support from the Protestant community, and many left the established churches to join them. This caused a drop in membership in ten of the largest Protestant denominations (groupings within the Church) during the late 1960s.

The Evangelical movement was much broader and more open than the Christian fundamentalist movement, and it had an international following through the World Evangelical Fellowship formed in 1951. Evangelicals regularly cooperated with Jews and Roman Catholics in their campaigns in defense of family values. Although the Evangelical movement contained many fundamentalists, it also had members with more liberal views on social issues. Some Evangelicals, while continuing to believe that the Bible was the word of God, became open to modern biblical criticism, and even accepted Darwin's controversial theory of evolution.

During the late 1970s and the 1980s, Christian fundamentalists abandoned their separatism, and began once more to engage themselves in the political and social debates of the day. Unlike earlier fundamentalists, who denied themselves luxuries, this new generation was not ashamed of making and spending money, and saw nothing sinful in fast cars and expensive clothing.

Carl McIntire (1907–2002)

Carl McIntire was a leading fundamentalist for more than fifty years. Unlike many Evangelicals McIntire remained true to the fundamentalist cause throughout his life, and never softened his message to appeal to people outside the movement. The main targets of his fierce rhetoric were Communism, **liberalism**, **racial integration**, sex education, and evolution. He reached his peak of popularity during the 1960s with his daily half-hour radio program, *Twentieth-Century Reformation Hour*, which was broadcast to six hundred stations in the United States and Canada.

In addition to their conservative views on issues of sex and relationships, the new fundamentalists became more outspoken on economic and political issues. They pressed for low taxation, reduced spending on welfare, and increased spending on defense. Since the beginning of the 1980s, it became difficult to separate the fundamentalists from the Evangelicals, and the two terms are now often used interchangeably.

Christian fundamentalists protesting outside a bookstore against the sale of what they consider pornography.

The Moral Majority

In the late 1970s, a new movement emerged uniting conservatives of all kinds, from Christian fundamentalists to Catholics and Jews. Its purpose was to encourage millions of ordinary conservative Americans to become involved in the political process. The movement was called the Moral Majority, and it was led by a popular fundamentalist preacher named Jerry Falwell. Through Falwell's television channel, campaign rallies, and mass mailings, thousands of people were persuaded to become politically active.

Voter registration drives brought many people who previously hadn't voted onto the electoral register. Voters were told about a politician's previous record on a range of issues important to religious conservatives—such as abortion, equal rights for women, and school prayer—and they were guided on which way to vote. In 1980 The Moral Majority helped Republican candidate Ronald Reagan win the U.S. presidency. However, some felt that once he was in office, Reagan did little to promote the fundamentalist agenda.

Televangelist Jim Bakker, founder of the PTL (Praise The Lord) network, with his former wife, Tammy Faye. In 1987 his adulterous affair with a church secretary became national news. In 1989 he was convicted of financial fraud and went to prison for five years.

Televangelism

In the early 1960s, the first Christian television networks appeared in the United States, creating a nationwide platform for Evangelical and fundamentalist preachers. Among the first preachers to see the potential of television were Billy Graham and Oral Roberts, an evangelist and faith healer who appeared to heal people live on television.

Televangelism reached its heyday in the early 1980s. By this time there were more than 100 religious programs on television, and the more successful ones were broadcast on 200 or more television stations around the country. Popular televangelists such as Jerry Falwell and Pat Robertson could reach millions with their programs, and this made them politically powerful. Much airtime was devoted to fundraising, and many televangelists became very wealthy as a result. Toward the end of the 1980s, a series of financial and sexual scandals involving televangelists threatened to tarnish the whole industry. However, the arrival of satellite and cable TV in the 1990s lowered the cost of airtime and gave religious broadcasting a new lease on life.

During the 1980s the conservatives dominated the political scene, and it became harder for the Moral Majority to find reasons to raise funds from its supporters. Having won the battle to control the government, their supporters saw less need to continue making donations. In 1987 Falwell dissolved the Moral Majority. His place as the nation's leading fundamentalist was taken by Pat Robertson, a **Pentecostal** minister and televangelist.

The Christian Coalition

Rather than trying to influence the political scene from the sidelines, Robertson decided to run for president himself in 1988, representing the conservative Republican Party. He had a huge base of support through his Christian Broadcasting Network, and access to plentiful funds. However, despite spending more money than any other candidate, Robertson failed to get any nominations from his own party to be the Republican presidential candidate. After this defeat, Robertson focused on building the Christian Coalition, an organization similar to the Moral Majority. By 1992 it claimed to have 350,000 members. During the 1990s the Christian Coalition tried hard to make the Republican Party more supportive of its beliefs

Pat Robertson campaigning for the U.S. presidency in 1988. Many fundamentalists were uncomfortable with his mixing of religion and politics. In one poll of conservative Christians, 42 percent said that his status as a former clergyman made them less likely to vote for him.

MARCH ON WASHINGTON
LESBIAN, GAY, & BI
RIGHTS & LIBERATION

on moral issues. It spent a lot of money backing candidates with conservative views, and managed to get several elected. However, Christian Coalition candidates failed in 1992, 1996, and 2000 to win the Republican nomination for the U.S. presidency.

A gay rights march in Washington, D.C. Christian fundamentalists are fiercely opposed to giving homosexuals the same rights as heterosexual couples, such as the right to marry or adopt children.

From an interview given by Jerry Falwell on September 14, 2001, three days after the terrorist attack on the World Trade Center in New York claimed thousands of lives:

"The ACLU [American Civil Liberties Union] has got to take a lot of blame for this. And I know I'll hear from them for this, but throwing God ... out of the public square, out of the schools, the abortionists have got to bear some burden for this because God will not be mocked, and when we destroy 40 million little innocent babies, we make God mad.... I really believe that the pagans and the abortionists and the feminists and the gays and the lesbians who are actively trying to make that an alternative lifestyle, the ACLU, People for the American Way, all of them who try to secularize America.... I point the thing in their face and say—you helped this happen."

The main aims of most modern Christian fundamentalists can be stated as follows: They want abortion and homosexuality banned; they want women to take up what they see as their traditional roles as wives and mothers; and in schools they want compulsory public prayer, the story of creation to be taught, and the teaching of evolution to be banned.

To achieve these aims, fundamentalists have raised and spent a lot of money, encouraged thousands to become politically active, supported election campaigns, **lobbied** politicians, and fought court cases. But so far their efforts have only been partially successful. Despite hard campaigning by the fundamentalists, abortion remains legal in the United States, although some states have laws that make abortions difficult to obtain.

In 1997 members of the Evangelical Christian group the Promise Keepers lie face down in prayer at a religious gathering in view of the Washington Monument in Washington, D.C.

Prayer in school—another regular campaigning issue for the fundamentalists—has been judged in some courts to be against the U.S. **constitution**. Evolution also continues to be taught in schools throughout the United States, despite numerous court cases in which fundamentalists have tried to argue that it should be banned or given equal classroom time with "**creation science**."

Individual liberty

Christian fundamentalism's failure to impose its views on society at large has a lot to do with the nature of the United States and its people. The United States is a democracy, containing many diverse cultures, and it is generally united around certain values, including the liberty of the individual and the separation of church and state. These values are at odds with the fundamentalists, who would like all Americans to accept their beliefs on how people should live, behave, and worship. While many Americans are very religious, it seems that many also want to keep religion a private matter.

Oral Roberts (1918–)

Oral Roberts was one of the most famous and controversial evangelical preachers of the 20th century. During the 1940s he began his "crusades for Christ," in which he set himself the target of "winning a million souls for Christ" each year. In 1954, he bought time on U.S. television to display his gift of faith healing. Many sick people did appear to be healed when he laid his hands on them. This led him into conflicts with the fundamentalists, who accused him of trivializing their cause. Roberts grew increasingly wealthy from fundraising campaigns supposedly for charitable causes. During the 1980s he claimed that Jesus had told him he would die if his supporters did not give him eight million dollars in the next twelve months. The money was apparently raised, and Roberts survived.

Oral Roberts has always been a controversial figure, even among fundamentalists—many of whom do not believe in his miracle cures.

Islamic Fundamentalism

Islamic fundamentalism has several characteristics in common with Christian fundamentalism. Islamists, as the fundamentalists prefer to call themselves, choose to interpret their holy book, the **Qur'an,** literally. They wish to enforce the laws contained in the Qur'an, known as the *shari'ah*, on Islamic society. They are strict about the laws that forbid the drinking of alcohol and believe that women should not work or be educated and should wear a veil in public.

Muslims gather for prayers in Delhi, India, at the festival of Eid ul-Fitr, marking the end of Ramadan, the month of fasting.

Islamists reject many of the traditions and customs that developed within Islam during the Medieval period as a betrayal of the true faith. Much like Christian fundamentalists, they wish to return to a purer form of their religion, as it existed in its earliest days. Like the Evangelicals, Islamists emphasize the importance of being "converted" to true Islam, and they believe in the importance of **missionary** work.

Islamic fundamentalists are not all the same. Some, like the Saudi-born terrorist Osama bin Laden, believe in bringing together all Muslim peoples in a restoration of the **caliphate**—a united Islamic world under one central leadership. Others, like the Palestinian organization Hamas, wish to create an Islamic republic in just one country—in their case, Palestine. In fundamentalist Iran women drive cars and go to work, whereas in Afghanistan, under the fundamentalist Taliban regime (1995-2001), women had no such rights. There are different kinds of fundamentalism in Islam, but there are also enough similarities to discuss it as a single movement.

What is Islam?

Islam was founded by an Arabian merchant named Muhammad in the
seventh century C.E. Muslims believe that Muhammad was the last in a line
of prophets, such as Moses and Jesus, whose message came straight from
God (*Allah* in Arabic). They believe that Allah passed on his message to
Muhammad in the words of the Qur'an, the holy scripture of Islam. The
Qur'an contains teachings about God, justice, and daily life, as well as
Islamic versions of stories also found in the **Bible**. Muslims express their
faith in actions carried out each day, for example by praying five times a day,
fasting during the Muslim month of **Ramadan**, and going on a pilgrimage to
the holy city of Mecca at least once in a lifetime. Islam influences how
believers eat, dress, and behave. For example, Muslims don't eat pork and
can only eat meat slaughtered in a certain way. They cannot drink alcohol
or gamble, and they must dress modestly.

The origins of Islamic fundamentalism

From time to time in its development, Islam has faced crises, and these have usually been followed by attempts to return Islamic society to its original principles based on the teachings of the **Qur'an.** These are called **revivalist movements.** The origins of Islamic fundamentalism lie in these attempts at revival.

The first of the important revivalist movements occurred in the late 1200s and early 1300s, and was inspired by the teachings of Ahmad ibn Taymiyya (1263–1328). He was born soon after the invasion of the Middle East (where Arab Muslims lived) by an Asian people called the Mongols.

Different traditions of Islam

During the mid-seventh century, a division occurred in Islam when Ali, who was Muhammad's son-in-law, became the fourth **caliph** (ruler). One group, the Shi'a, meaning "followers," believed Ali was Muhammad's first true successor, because of his family relationship to the prophet. Another group, the Sunni, meaning "majority," disagreed. To this day, the Shi'a believe that the **caliphate** should be hereditary, like a dynasty of kings, whereas the Sunni insist that caliphs should be chosen democratically.

From about the 700s, a more mystical tradition arose in Islam, which became known as Sufism. This tradition emphasized the spiritual side of the faith. Unlike other forms of Islam, the Sufis used music and dance as part of their worship. Many different Sufi orders arose, some of which still survive today.

Taymiyya believed that the defeat by the Mongols had occurred because the Arab people had lost touch with Islamic teachings and had become corrupt. He objected to Sufism, for example, a more mystical form of Islam that emphasized the spiritual side of worship. Taymiyya insisted that all such "un-Islamic" traditions should cease, and that the Muslim world should be run according to the strict interpretation of Islamic law as it appears in the Qur'an.

Wahhabism

By the 1700s century, the Arab world was dominated by the powerful **Ottoman Empire**, which occupied lands in southern Europe, North Africa, the Middle East, and Asia. The Ottoman rulers called themselves caliphs, using the ancient title to give themselves religious authority over the people of their empire. But Sufism was flourishing in many parts of the empire, and many Arabs believed that the Ottoman caliphate was corrupt.

A painting of the fourth caliph, Ali, who was Muhammad's son-in-law. Shi'a Muslims, such as most of those who live in Iran, believe that Ali was Muhammad's first true successor.

Muhammad ibn 'Abd al-Wahhab (1703–1792)

Al-Wahhab was born near Riyadh in modern-day Saudi Arabia. He was a bright child, and at the age of ten could recite the whole of the Qur'an from memory. After completing his education at Medina, he lived abroad for many years. On his travels around the Islamic world, al-Wahhab found evidence of differing religious practices, which he viewed as a corruption of the original faith. While a teacher in Iran in 1736, al-Wahhab began to spread his belief about a return to a purer form of Islam. On his return to Medina, he wrote the *Kitab at-tawhid* (Book of Unity), which became the main text of the Wahhabi movement. In 1745 he met with Prince Muhammad ibn Sa'ud, who was impressed with al-Wahhab's ideas, and adopted them for his country, Saudi Arabia.

A movement arose in Saudi Arabia known as the **Wahhabis,** after its founder, Muhammad al-Wahhab. The Wahhabis were opposed to Sufism and Shi'ism, and sought a return to a purer and more traditional interpretation of the **Qur'an.** In contrast with the Sufis, the Wahhabis insisted that Allah stood apart from the world and could not be reached through mystical rituals or meditation. They also demanded independence from the **caliphate.**

Saudi forces carrying the Wahhabi standard in the Arabian desert in 1913. That year they captured the Hasa region of the Arabian peninsula, as part of their campaign to spread Wahhabism to the whole of Arabia.

Major concerns of the Wahhabis were progress and change. They believed that the innovations of the modern world—such as the introduction of coffee, tobacco, and printing—endangered the purity of their religion. They looked back on the "golden age" of Muhammad's time as an ideal period, and they wished to preserve Islamic society as it was then. In their desire to purge Islam of new and foreign influences, the Wahhabis were very similar to modern Islamic fundamentalists, and can be seen as one of the major inspirations for today's movement. Al-Wahhab's teachings were adopted by the Muslim leader and founder of Saudi Arabia, ibn Sa'ud, and **Wahhabism** was spread by conquest to most of Arabia. This strict form of Islam has been the dominant faith in Saudi Arabia since 1800, making Saudi Arabia arguably the world's first Islamic fundamentalist state.

Alexandria in Egypt under British colonial rule (1883-1937). During this period Egyptian Islamic courts declined in power, and were only permitted to deal with cases involving personal relationships.

The Islamic Movement

During the late 1800s and 1900s, the Ottoman Empire declined, and European powers, fueled by the wealth of the **Industrial Revolution**, grew to dominate many parts of the Muslim world. The conquering of Arabs by European powers led to a steady wearing away of Islamic identity.

The introduction of Western goods, such as modern weapons, railroads, and later electricity, running water, and cars, gave many Muslims a taste for Western life and culture. European-style institutions, such as law courts, banks, schools, and colleges, were introduced in many countries of the **Ottoman Empire,** in parallel with existing religious institutions. For the most part, these reforms were carried out by local rulers.

This process of Westernization was opposed by some in religious circles and led, in the 1870s, to a new upsurge in Islamic revivalism. One of the leading figures in this new movement was Jamal al-Afghani (1838–1897). Al-Afghani traveled throughout the Islamic world, spreading his anti-Western message. He believed that Western powers like Britain, France, and Russia were working with Middle Eastern rulers to exploit the Muslim people and the resources of their countries.

Muhammad Abduh (1849–1905)

Abduh is regarded as one of the major influences behind the modern revival of Islam. In 1899 he was made the official expert in Islamic law in Egypt, and in this position he brought about many reforms. In his writings and actions, Abduh opposed the blind acceptance of traditional customs, and urged a return to the pure faith of early Islam. He called for modernization based on Islamic principles. For example, he believed that girls, as well as boys, should have the right to an education. He also argued that there was nothing un-Islamic about Western technology, so long as it was put to good use.

Muhammad Abduh as a young man. When he was a student, Abduh became involved in the Islamic Movement. He was exiled from Egypt for six years after taking part in a rebellion against the British in 1882.

In an effort to unite the Muslim world, al-Afghani formed the Islamic Movement. He encouraged the strict observance of Islamic beliefs in everyday life and the reintroduction of *shari'ah*—Islamic law. *Shari'ah* law arises from the teachings of the **Qur'an,** the **Hadith** (the sayings of Muhammad), and the interpretations of scholars. It is both a personal code for every Muslim, and a system of law governing strict Muslim countries. Al-Afghani also urged Muslims to fight the Western powers, if necessary with the modern weapons and technology the Europeans had introduced. The Islamic Movement aimed to restore the power and status that Islam had enjoyed during the height of the Ottoman Empire. Modern Islamic fundamentalism dates from this time, and is a reaction to the threat of Western economic and cultural domination.

The Ottoman Empire collapsed in 1918, following its defeat in the First World War. The **caliphate** ended, and the Islamic world found itself without an overall leader. Many territories of the former empire, including Iraq, Jordan, Lebanon, Palestine, and Syria fell under the control of France and Britain. In other places, such as Turkey, Egypt, and Iran, independent nations were formed. Here, the new leaders were modernizers who wished to follow the West and reduce the role of religion. They separated Islam from the state and replaced religious institutions with **secular** ones.

Al-Afghani, founder of the Islamic Movement, was concerned about the influence of Western materialism on Islam. In 1880 he wrote:

"They [the materialists, influenced by the West] are the destroyers of civilization and the corrupters of morals.... Their kindness is a ruse, their truthfulness a deceit, their claim to humanity imaginary, and their call to science and knowledge a snare and a forgery. They make trustworthiness into treachery; will not keep a secret; and will sell their closest friend for a copper coin. They are slaves to the belly and bound by lust.... Thus, from all we have expounded, it becomes clear ... that religion, even if it be false and the basest of religions ... is better than the way of the materialists.... The Islamic religion is the only religion that ... sets up proofs for each fundamental belief in such a way that it will be useful to all people."

The Muslim Brotherhood

In the period following the collapse of the Ottoman Empire, various Islamic groups formed to oppose Western dominance and the reforms of the modernizers. One group, which was to have lasting impact, was the Muslim Brotherhood, founded in Egypt in 1928 by Hasan al-Banna. It urged a return to the **Qur'an** and the **Hadith** as guides to a successful modern Islamic society. The Brotherhood spread quickly through Egypt, the Sudan, Syria, Palestine, and Lebanon, encouraging these areas to readopt strict Islamic law.

During the 1950s leaders of Middle Eastern countries, such as President Nasser of Egypt, discouraged Islamic revivalism. Instead they tried to promote Arab **nationalism**—a sense of identification with Arabic culture (the Arabs are a people living throughout North Africa and the Middle East). The idea was that, if all the Arab nations worked together, they could be strong enough to oppose the West. Communism also became increasingly popular among Arabs at this time, many of whom saw an alliance with the Communist Soviet Union as another way to end Western influence.

However, movements such as the Muslim Brotherhood kept the flame of Islamic revivalism burning during this period. One of the Brotherhood's leaders was Sayyid Qutb (1906–1966). His writings in the early 1960s—especially *In the Shadow of the Qur'an* and *Milestones*—were to be a major influence on radical Muslims in the years to come.

Qutb differed from earlier Islamic thinkers and from many of his

In *Milestones* Sayyid Qutb wrote:

"The faithful Muslim seeks a state where there is no sovereignty [authority] except God's, no law except from God, and no authority of one man over another, as the authority in all respects belongs to God."

contemporaries in his view that there was no such thing as Islamic society in today's world. He believed that, since the time of the Prophet, the world had deteriorated into a state of *jahiliyya*, or ignorance. It was the duty of every Muslim to break free of the world, then destroy it, and build a pure Islamic state on its ruins. Qutb was executed by the Egyptian government in 1966 for his political activities.

Qutb's belief that violence was a necessary step toward the creation of a pure Islamic state was later taken up by fellow Egyptian, Abd al-Salam Faraj. Faraj took the Arabic word **jihad**, meaning "struggle," and redefined it as "violent struggle" or "holy war." He said it was the duty of Muslims to engage in violence against the enemies of Islam. Their reward for doing so would be a place in paradise. Faraj was later executed for his part in the 1981 assassination of President Anwar Sadat of Egypt.

Two imprisoned Islamic militants, accused of the October 1981 assassination of Egyptian President Anwar Sadat, defiantly hold up copies of the Qur'an. They were executed in April 1982, along with three others.

The Palestinian issue

In 1948 the UN established the Jewish state of Israel in the former British territory of Palestine. A war immediately erupted between the new nation and neighboring Arab states opposed to its establishment. Many hundreds of thousands of Palestinian Arabs fled their homes. They settled in refugee camps in Syria, Lebanon, Jordan, and in territories bordering Israel known as the West Bank and the Gaza Strip. With its birth, Israel aroused the hostility of the Arab world. The Arabs were angered by the displacement of the Palestinians from their homeland, and the occupation by a Jewish state of formerly Arab lands and Muslim holy sites. In 1967, in what became known as the Six Day War, Israel defeated a combined Arab attack. As a result of that war, Israel expanded its territory to include the West Bank and the Gaza Strip. These areas became known as the "occupied territories."

An Israeli soldier with an Arab prisoner during the 1967 Six Day War. Israel scored a dramatic victory, despite facing simultaneous attack on three fronts by Egypt, Syria, and Jordan. The legacy of this brief conflict casts a shadow over the Middle East to this day.

The war, and the subsequent enlargement of Israel, caused widespread anger throughout the Muslim world, and many took up the cause of Palestinian liberation. A group of **militant** Palestinians called the Palestine Liberation Organization (PLO) turned to terrorism in its desire to destroy Israel.

From about 1973 Islamic revivalism, as defined by al-Afghani, Qutb, and other thinkers, began to replace **nationalism** and Communism as the most influential radical movement of the Muslim world. The PLO was a secular organization, so militant Islamic Palestinians in the occupied territories formed their own anti-Israeli terrorist groups. Most notable among these was Hamas (the Islamic Resistance Movement), formed in 1978.

The Iranian revolution

In Iran during the late 1970s, the pro-Western, secular government of Shah Mohammad Reza Pahlavi faced fierce opposition from the country's religious leaders, known as the *ayatollahs*. Iranian Muslims followed the minority Shi'ite tradition of Islam, and were not regarded as true Muslims by the Sunni, who form the majority of Muslims worldwide (see page 28). Nevertheless, Iran provided the setting in 1979 for a revolution that would shock the world and begin the major upsurge known as Islamic fundamentalism that continues to this day.

A pro-Khomeini demonstration at the time of the Iranian Revolution. The revolution succeeded partly because the Shah's government had never been able to suppress the Islamists as other Arab governments had managed. The ayatollahs were also fortunate that the Shah's program of modernization failed to improve the lives of Iranians.

In 1978 there were riots and demonstrations throughout Iran. In January 1979 the Shah left the country. The opposition movements united under a new leader, Ayatollah Khomeini, then in exile, who took power in February. Khomeini ruthlessly imposed *shari'ah* law (see page 26). All aspects of life, from marriage ceremonies to banking, were made to conform to *shari'ah*. Once their power was consolidated in Iran, the *ayatollahs* tried to export their revolution to neighboring countries. Iraq, with its large Shi'ite minority, was their first target. However, after a bloody eight-year war (1980–1988), Iran finally withdrew.

Members of the terrorist group Hezbollah lined up behind Shi'ite clerics.

Hezbollah

The Iranian fundamentalists also tried unsuccessfully to spark Islamic revolutions in Lebanon, Egypt, Saudi Arabia, Jordan, and Algeria. In Lebanon, the Iranians gave their support to a Shi'ite group known as Hezbollah (the "Party of Allah"). The aim of this group was to conquer Lebanon, and ultimately to create one all-encompassing Islamic state. Hezbollah were among the most single-minded and ruthless of Islamic fundamentalists, willing to give up their lives to kill their enemies. For example, in October 1983,

The Rushdie fatwah

In 1989 Ayatollah Khomeini issued a *fatwah* (religious ruling) that sentenced the Anglo-Indian writer Salman Rushdie to death for blasphemy (showing disrespect to God). This *fatwah* was in response to Rushdie's novel, *The Satanic Verses*, which contains a passage about the birth of a religion resembling Islam that many Muslims find offensive. Rushdie was forced to go into hiding in case a Muslim decided to carry out the death sentence against him. In 1999 the Iranian government pledged not to continue the *fatwah*. But in 2000 an extremist Iranian group, the Iranian 15th Khordad Foundation, offered a bounty of $2.8 million for Rushdie's execution. And in February 2001, the Islamic Propagation Organization reaffirmed the death sentence on Rushdie. President Khatami of Iran accused these groups of damaging the country's international image. In March 2002 Air Canada banned Salman Rushdie from its flights, saying that the extra security required for him to fly could mean delays of up to three hours for other passengers.

a Hezbollah suicide bomber drove a truck filled with explosives into a barracks in Beirut, killing 241 U.S. Marines and 58 French paratroopers.

The Iranians had shown how an Islamic revolution could occur. Their success inspired Islamic militants throughout the world. The 1980s and 1990s were times of **radicalism** and violence in many Muslim countries, from North Africa to southeast Asia, as increasing numbers of young, eager, and committed Muslims flocked to the cause.

In Egypt and Algeria, the fundamentalist movements were suppressed, while in Jordan and Pakistan fundamentalist candidates were allowed to compete in elections. In 1989 a fundamentalist regime came to power in Sudan, and another—the Taliban—took control of Afghanistan in 1995, but these were isolated successes. In most cases the fundamentalists, for all their ruthlessness and commitment, have been unable to achieve real political power.

Anti-Americanism

The upsurge of modern Islamic militancy has many causes. They include the political and economic failures of the post-independence Arab governments, the Palestinian issue, and the inspirational writings of men such as Sayyid Qutb. But perhaps the most potent force driving Islamic fundamentalism today is anti-Americanism. This is reflected in an increasing number of attacks by Islamic terrorists on American targets. The worst of these were the attacks on September 11, 2001, when aircrafts full of innocent passengers were hijacked by members of the terrorist group Al Qaeda, and deliberately flown into the twin towers of the World Trade Center in New York and the Pentagon near Washington, D.C. More than 3,000 people were killed.

There are several reasons why the United States has attracted such hatred. As the leading Western power, it has become the modern-day equivalent of the European colonial powers of the 1800s (see pages 31–32). Although it has no direct political control over the Islamic world, the United States's influence is felt in terms of its economic power and its ability to persuade the governments of Muslim countries to act in America's interests.

The Taliban

The Taliban regime in Afghanistan (1995–2001) was notable for its extreme fundamentalist policies. Its members wished to create the world's purest Islamic state, and set about banning all "corrupting" influences such as TV, music, and movies. They followed a strict interpretation of *shari'ah* law. Women in particular faced extreme restrictions: they were denied education or the right to work, and were forced to cover themselves from head to foot in a garment called a **burka**. Adultery was punishable by stoning to death, and the hands and feet of thieves were amputated. Those who did not pray five times a day or fast during the Muslim holy month of Ramadan were sent to prison.

Muslims also feel their culture is under threat from the worldwide dominance of American culture, conveyed in the form of movies, television, music, books, food, and fashion. They are offended by Western liberal attitudes toward sex, alcohol, drugs, and **gender roles**. They view this culture as corrupt, decadent, and completely at odds with Islamic principles. They are also angered by the willingness of their own governments to be corrupted by American culture.

Many Muslims are also enraged by the United States's policy in the Middle East, especially its support of Israel. Another cause of discontent among religious Muslims is the presence, since 1991, of U.S. troops in the holy land of Saudi Arabia. This has been a particular source of outrage for the Saudi-born terrorist, Osama bin Laden, who masterminded the September 11, 2001, attacks. Bin Laden has called upon Muslims to kill Americans—even civilians—for as long as their soldiers remain in Saudi Arabia.

On September 11, 2001, the second hijacked plane crashes into the south tower of the World Trade Center in New York. The gaping hole in the north tower from the earlier collision can clearly be seen. Soon afterward both towers collapsed.

A statement made by Osama bin Laden in 1998 contained the following words:

"Nothing is more sacred than belief except repulsing an enemy who is attacking religion and life. On that basis, and in compliance with God's order, we issue the following fatwah to all Muslims. The ruling to kill the Americans and their allies—civilians and military—is an individual duty for every Muslim who can do it in any country in which it is possible to do it."

Muslim women in Jakarta, Indonesia, demonstrate their support for the introduction of Islamic *shari'ah* law in August 2002.

Islamic fundamentalism today

Since 1979 Islamic fundamentalism has been a major force for change around the world. It is a cause that has been taken up enthusiastically by young Muslims everywhere, from Bradford in England to Mindanao in the Philippines. In many parts of the Middle East and central and southern Asia, Islamic fundamentalism has had a violent aspect, and caused political instability.

Islam itself is not a violent religion. A substantial number of Islamists are opposed to terrorist violence of any kind. Islamism, or Islamic revivalism, is seen by many in the Muslim world as a positive force. Groups like the Muslim Brotherhood, although they have been involved with terrorism in the past, are now pursuing their aims by winning power through **democratic** elections. Islamists often see their role as trying to influence Islamic governments toward implementing Islamic laws, and bringing those who have deviated back to the true faith. Despite this, Islamic fundamentalism has become strongly associated with terrorism in the Western mind, because it is violent fundamentalist groups such as Hamas, Hezbollah, and Palestinian Islamic Jihad that make the headlines.

Osama bin Laden (1957–)

The son of a wealthy Saudi Arabian businessman, bin Laden developed an early interest in Islam. At the age of 23 he went to help in the resistance to the Soviet invasion of Afghanistan in 1979–1988. He fought with the Mujahedeen, a guerilla force supported in part by the United States. At this time he developed a large network of Islamic militants, which later evolved into the international terrorist group, Al Qaeda.

In the early 1990s, bin Laden's increasingly extreme views brought him into conflict with the Saudi regime. He moved to Sudan, where he sponsored Islamic terrorist attacks around the world, especially against Saudi and American targets. In 1995, he moved his operation to Afghanistan where Al Qaeda allied itself with the ruling Taliban regime. After the September 11, 2001, attacks by Al Qaeda members, American-led forces toppled the Taliban and destroyed Al Qaeda's bases, although they failed to find bin Laden.

Most Muslims disagree with bin Laden's violent interpretation of Islam. However, his uncompromising attitude appeals to the poor and frustrated throughout the Islamic world. He is willing to cut across the boundaries that divide many Muslims. For example, despite being a Sunni, he made an alliance with the Shi'ite terrorist group, Hezbollah. His ultimate aim is to reestablish the **caliphate** and unite Islam into one force. Then, he believes, Islam will be strong enough to defeat the West.

Osama bin Laden's hostility toward the United States has made him popular among thousands of Islamic militantsworldwide. An audiotape containing what some experts believe to be his voice, released in November 2002, suggests that he may still be alive.

Other Forms of Fundamentalism

The long conflict with the Palestinians and Arab nations that has followed the establishment of the state of Israel has affected Jewish people in different ways. Many yearn for a peaceful settlement with the Palestinians, even if that means giving some land back to them. There are others who will accept nothing less than outright victory over the Arabs and refuse to give up an inch of land. The latter group include a religious movement of mainly Israeli Jews who have become known as Jewish fundamentalists.

Jewish fundamentalism

For many centuries, the Jews were without a homeland. In the 1500s and 1600s, a movement known as **Zionism** emerged, arguing that the Jews should reclaim the land they had possessed in Biblical times. In the 1800s and the twentieth century, Zionism became a stronger political movement as it sought to create a **secular** Jewish state.

Yet in the decades since Israel was founded, most fundamentalist Jews have come to view its establishment in religious terms. They see the current **secular** state of Israel as the initial form of the religious "land of Israel" (*Eretz Yisrael* in Hebrew), which would be governed according to *halakah* (Jewish law). For confirmation of this view, fundamentalists look to the Jewish holy book, the **Torah**, where there is a commandment to return to *Eretz Yisrael*, to settle there and conquer it.

Jewish Zionists believe they have the right to settle anywhere in the occupied territory of the West Bank, which they call by the Biblical names of Judea and Samaria. Many of them carry guns and there are frequent violent clashes with Palestinians.

Gush Emunim

Gush Emunim (the Bloc of the Faithful) was a religious Zionist group formed in 1974. The members of this group believed that Israel's 1967 territorial conquests were willed by God, and they were determined that not one inch should be given back. While the Israeli government was facing international pressure to return some of this land to the Palestinians, Gush began settling in the occupied territories in an attempt to make them a permanent part of Israel. During the late 1970s, Gush Emunim became increasingly popular in Israel, and Gush leaders were elected to the Israeli Parliament. Then, when the Israeli government made a peace deal with Egypt and began handing back land, Gush turned to terrorism, wounding two Palestinian mayors in car bomb attacks in the West Bank in 1980. Another plot to dynamite the **mosques** on a Jewish holy site in Jerusalem was discovered, and in 1984 several Gush members were arrested.

Their view, which is known as religious Zionism, became more popular after Israel's unexpected victory in the 1967 war. As a result, Israel drove back the Arabs and greatly expanded its territory, bringing it roughly into line with the borders of the biblical land of Israel. To religious Zionists, it appeared that God's will had been done.

Gush Emunim planned to blow up these mosques on the Temple Mount in Jerusalem.

The religious Zionists, with their belief in Israel's God-given status, are the driving force behind the movement by Jewish people to settle the occupied territories. Fundamentalists see this not as conquest, but as the reclamation of land that rightfully belongs to them.

Unlike their Muslim and Christian counterparts, Jewish fundamentalists do not seek converts to their extreme cause, except among other Jews. One reason why Jewish fundamentalists do not try to convert non-Jews is that many of them hold racist views toward non-Jews. They regard Jews as superior to Arabs and Christians. This belief stems partly from a Jewish movement, popular between the 1500s and 1800s, called the Lurianic Cabbala. One of the main beliefs of this movement was that the world was created solely for the Jews, and that non-Jews have "satanic souls."

Jewish settlers from Elon Moreh, near Nablus, carry the body of Rabbi Hillel Lieberman, who was killed in October 2000, probably by Palestinians. Despite the violence, the numbers of Jewish settlers continues to grow at a rate of 5 percent a year.

Their racist attitudes mean that many Jewish fundamentalists are not troubled by the idea of settling on land previously lived on by Arabs. Some, such as the extremist followers of the **Rabbi** Meir Cahane (who died in 1990), would like to evict Arabs from land in the Middle East that they believe rightfully belongs to Jews. A few even believe that Jews who kill Arabs should not be punished. In February 1994 the Jewish extremist Baruch Goldstein fired his rifle indiscriminately at a crowd of Palestinian worshipers in the Tomb of the Patriarchs in the town of Hebron, killing 29 people. Yet a number of fundamentalists refused to condemn this act as murder.

Jewish fundamentalists justify their acts of violence—even attacks on fellow Jews—by reference to their scriptures. In November 1995 a Jewish fundamentalist named Yigal Amir assassinated the Israeli prime minister Yitzhak Rabin, who had recently signed a peace deal with the Palestinians. Amir claimed his action was justified by the "law of the pursuer," from the **Talmud** (the book of Jewish law). This law commands every Jew to kill or wound any other Jew who is perceived as intending to kill another Jew. Since, in Amir's view, Rabin was endangering Israel and therefore the lives of Jewish people by his peace deal, Amir felt it was right to kill him. Amir was sentenced to life in prison.

Rabbi Kook the Elder, the father of religious Zionism, said:

"The difference between a Jewish soul and souls of non-Jews—all of them in all different levels—is greater and deeper than the difference between a human soul and the souls of cattle."

Quoted in Israel Shahak and Norton Mezvinsky, *Jewish Fundamentalism in Israel.*

Yigal Amir, assassin of Yitzhak Rabin, under arrest. At his trial, Amir said in his defense that Rabin had wanted to "give our country to the Arabs." "We need to be coldhearted," he added.

Hindu fundamentalism

Hindu fundamentalism differs from other forms of fundamentalism because of the differing nature of the religion. Hindus believe in many gods; they are tolerant of other faiths, and respect their gods. They have several holy books, such as the Vedas, the Bhaghavad Gita, and the Ramayana, and do not insist that one book should be regarded as the complete source of truth and wisdom.

Hindu fundamentalists therefore do not claim that there is one literally true sacred text. However, they are less tolerant of other faiths than are the majority of Hindus. They believe that India—where 80 percent of the population is Hindu—should remain Hindu, and are pushing for a change in the **constitution** to limit the freedom to practice other religions.

Hindu fundamentalism experienced an upsurge in the late 1980s. Many Hindus were concerned about the rise of other religions in India, such as Christianity, Islam, Buddhism, and Sikhism. They opposed **secularism**, a policy followed by Indian governments for the sake of the religious minorities of India, and

"Increasing intolerance among the Hindu fundamentalist organizations, which pose a grave threat to democracy, are an indication of the rise of fascist forces in India. What happened with European fascism is now happening with Hindus."

M. Mohanty, Professor of Politics, Delhi University, February 2000.

The Dalit

The policy of secularism also threatened the Hindu **caste** system. Under this system people are born into a certain rank in society, depending on the caste (or social grouping) of their family, and this cannot be changed. The lowest ranked caste are the Dalit, or Oppressed. They have few rights or legal protection, and many are forced to live separately from other Hindus. There have been several cases since 1990 where Hindu fundamentalists have shown their "superiority" over the Dalit by mistreating and even killing them.

wished to create a truly Hindu nation, or *Hindu Rashtra*.

In 1992 in the northern Indian town of Ayodhya, a 16th-century Muslim mosque, believed to have been built on the site of a Hindu temple, was destroyed by Hindu fundamentalists. The Vishwa Hindu Parishad, a Hindu fundamentalist organization, then led a campaign to build a Hindu temple on the site, causing further anguish to the Muslim community.

In 1999 a Hindu fundamentalist party, the Bharatiya Janata Party (BJP) took power in India. The BJP had previously supported a policy of Hindutva (the establishment of a Hindu state). However, since forming the government, the party has presented a more moderate image to the public. Despite its new image, the BJP has introduced policies to make Indian education more Hindu-based, and history books have been rewritten to emphasize India's Hindu past.

Hindu fundamentalists hold a news conference to publicize their plans to build a temple on the site of the razed mosque at Ayodhya, India.

Buddhist fundamentalism

Buddhism is practiced mainly in southeast Asia, as well as by many people in the West. It is a peaceful faith, preaching kindness and compassion to fellow human beings, and it has no single sacred text that serves as a guide to life. Despite this, an intolerant, fundamentalist form of Buddhism emerged in the 20th century. The two main locations of Buddhist fundamentalism are Bhutan in the eastern Himalayas and Sri Lanka.

In Bhutan the state religion is Buddhism. The ruling monarchy has adopted a very strict and historical form of Buddhism. The king, who shares power with Bhutan's Buddhist monks, has reinterpreted the **Dharma**, or spiritual laws of Buddhism, as a way of strengthening his own authority. He has followed a policy of purging Bhutan of foreign cultures and non-Buddhist religions. The Hindus of southern Bhutan have been forced to adopt Buddhist traditions and culture. In the 1990s they suffered imprisonment and torture for trying to demand equal rights.

On the island of Sri Lanka, Buddhist fundamentalism is practiced by the Sinhalese people, who form the majority of the population. In a similar way to the Bhutanese monarchy, the Sinhalese have used Buddhism as a means of reinforcing their power and dominance on the island. Sinhala-Buddhist fundamentalism has proved a mixed blessing for Sri Lanka. It has strengthened Sri Lanka's sense of national identity, but it has also brought conflict between the Sinhalese and the Tamils, an **ethnic minority** in the northeast of the island.

Sikh fundamentalism

The Sikh faith began in India in the 1400s. It includes elements of both Hinduism and Islam, yet

A Sinhalese Buddhist monk. Buddhism has been Sri Lanka's main religion since the third century B.C.E. Buddhist fundamentalists believe that Sri Lanka is destined to be the island of the Dharma, or Buddhist teachings.

it is different from both. Sikhs believe in one god called *Waheguru*, meaning "Great Teacher." Equality of all people lies at the heart of their faith, and Sikhs place great emphasis on giving to the poor.

Sikh fundamentalism emerged in 1981, mainly in response to attacks on the Sikh community in India. The movement was led by a Sikh priest named Bhindranwale, who believed in a traditional form of Sikhism, and pressured the Indian government for a separate Sikh state. Bhindranwale and many others died in an Indian attack on the Sikh Golden Temple in Amritsar in 1984. Since then, some Sikh fundamentalists have carried out terrorist attacks against Indian leaders, including kidnappings, bombings, and assassinations. Sikh fundamentalists do not seek converts, and most of their energy is focused on keeping their identity and fighting for an independent nation.

Sant Jarnail Singh Bhindranwale (1947–1984)

Bhindranwale trained in a Sikh religious school, becoming its head priest in 1971. He preached a strict form of a Sikhism, denouncing drink, drugs, and the trimming of hair. In the early 1980s, he campaigned for a separate Sikh state of Khalistan. This led to a violent Sikh-Hindu conflict in Punjab. Along with 500 armed followers, he took refuge in the Golden Temple at Amritsar. He was killed by Indian security forces when they stormed the temple.

Simranjit Singh Mann (second right), a Sikh political leader, was imprisoned under suspicion of masterminding the assassination of Indian prime minister Indira Gandhi.

Comparing Fundamentalisms

Islamic and Christian fundamentalism are undoubtedly the most powerful fundamentalist movements operating in the world today. This is partly because they are, in terms of numbers, the largest of the world's religions, and so statistically are bound to attract a higher number of extremist followers. Another major reason for the strength of these forms of fundamentalism is that Islam and Christianity are religions that aim to win over the whole world to their way of thinking. Although Judaism (the Jewish religion) also has one God, one sacred text, and one set of laws, there is no impulse in this religion to convert others, and therefore Jewish fundamentalism remains a small-scale movement.

Hinduism and Buddhism have never produced a fundamentalist movement on the scale of Islam or Christianity. This is because these religions have so many different forms—having been influenced by the local cultures of the different countries where they have taken root—and no single movement can realistically claim to represent the true form of either religion.

Catholics believe that the Pope is God's earthly representative. He interprets the laws and principles of the Bible and tells people how to apply them to their daily lives. This leaves little opportunity for separate fundamentalist movements within the Catholic Church.

While each fundamentalist movement has its own distinctive features, the movements share many similarities. One similarity is the timing of their most recent occurrences: there has been a noticeable upsurge in religious fundamentalism since about 1978. At the heart of all these movements is a rejection of the global trend toward **secularism**.

Attitudes toward democracy

Along with secularism, most fundamentalist movements also reject the idea of democracy—the rule of the people. They propose instead that countries should be ruled by religious leaders. Islamic and Jewish fundamentalists desire new states to be formed based on religious laws— the *shari'ah* and the *halakah* respectively—and the fundamentalist interpretations of these law systems.

Roman Catholics and fundamentalism

Why do we never hear about Catholic fundamentalists? The reason for this absence lies in the nature of the religion. In the Roman Catholic faith, it is the Pope and his advisors who interpret the will of God, and direct Church policy on different issues. By contrast Protestants and Muslims are encouraged to read the holy scriptures and interpret the will of God in their own way. This has led to a number of separate movements arising within these religions, including fundamentalist groups. There are certainly different shades of belief within Catholicism, from liberal to **conservative**. However, Catholics by definition must accept the authority of the Pope. A Catholic wishing to form a separate movement would first have to leave the Catholic Church.

In the Philippines armed members of the Muslim fundamentalist group Abu Sayyaf pose for a photograph.

53

Hindu fundamentalists wish to impose a strict interpretation of Hinduism that would give few rights to members of the lower **castes**. Buddhism has been reinterpreted by its fundamentalist supporters to imply the absolute authority of the king, and Sikh fundamentalists have also adopted a very strict and intolerant form of Sikhism that they would be likely to impose on any future Sikh state.

The Sikh fundamentalist leader Bhindranwale justified the use of violence with the following saying:
"For a Sikh it is a sin to keep weapons and kill anyone, but it is an even greater sin to have weapons and not to seek justice."

American Christian fundamentalists, by contrast, accept the **democratic** system of the United States, and do not argue for its overthrow. There is no Christian equivalent of the *shari'ah* or the **halakah** that they would seek to impose in place of the U.S. **constitution**. They wish instead to defeat **secularism** and bring religion back into public life through legal and democratic means. However, many Christian fundamentalist policies are, by their nature, undemocratic because they seek to restrict the rights of certain groups in American society. For example, they wish to ban homosexuality, and want to forbid the teaching of evolution by biology teachers in even public schools.

Attitudes toward violence

At the heart of most of the world's religions are messages of love, peace, and goodwill. Yet religious fundamentalists have always found ways to justify the use of violence. The level of violence that fundamentalists use varies greatly according to their cultural background and the particular circumstances they find themselves in. Christian fundamentalists generally operate within an established democracy, such as the United States, where they are given plentiful opportunities to press their case without resorting to acts of violence. Among such groups, violence is therefore comparatively rare.

Among Muslim nations, however, there is only one democracy (Turkey), and Islamic fundamentalists, lacking other means of expressing themselves, often resort to bullets and bombs. Israel is a democracy, but one that has been under threat of attack from hostile neighbors for the whole of its short existence. This violence may be responsible, in part, for the violence of the Jewish fundamentalists who live there.

Both Sikh and Hindu traditions allow violence to be used in situations of self-defense. Hindu fundamentalists use the argument that they are defending their religion and culture from outside threats. One of the first acts of the fundamentalist BJP when it came to government in India in 1999 was to detonate a nuclear bomb to demonstrate the extent of its power.

Sikh boys with blue turbans and curved swords. Sikhs emphasize the importance of defending their religion. The swords and turbans remind Sikhs that they must be ready to fight for their faith.

The Future of Fundamentalism

For as long as there are people who wish to apply the teachings of the scriptures to their daily lives, and try to make others do so as well, fundamentalism will continue to exist. What is not clear, however, is if fundamentalism will always remain on the sidelines, or if it will one day take center stage.

Protest movement or future government?
American society is now firmly multiethnic and multireligious, with values of tolerance that reflect this, and women and homosexuals will not be persuaded to give up the rights and freedoms they have fought so hard to win. The Christian

Supporters hold up a placard of Mohammad Khatami, Iran's moderate, reformist president, during an election rally in February 2000. The fundamentalist rulers of Iran suffered a major defeat in that election, when reformists won control of the Iranian parliament.

Fundamentalist Christianity in Africa

The 20th century witnessed a shift of Christianity from being a religion practised by a majority of white people, to being followed by a nonwhite majority. In the early 21st century, more than 60 percent of Christians are from Africa, Asia, and Latin America. This has come about largely through the **missionary** efforts of the Evangelical Protestant church. It is possible that these places may prove a future source for Christian fundamentalism.

fundamentalists have instead resigned themselves to the status of a protest group, campaigning and demonstrating on specific issues and concerns.

Islamic fundamentalism is likely to remain a considerable force in Muslim societies. However, the chances are it will not succeed in its overall objective, which is the overthrow of nations and the reestablishment of the **caliphate**. The idea of the nation has proved a strong one, and even in places where fundamentalists have taken power, they have failed in their attempts to export the revolution to Muslims in other countries.

Islamic fundamentalism has faced several setbacks since the mid-1990s. In Iran the strict regime of the *ayatollahs* became increasingly unpopular, leading to the election of a moderate government in 1997. In Sudan the government's leading fundamentalist, Hassan al-Turabi, was forced out of office in 2000. The fundamentalist Wahhabi monarchy in Saudi Arabia has faced calls for greater freedom and democracy from human rights groups, such as the Saudi Committee for the Defense of Legitimate Rights (SCDLR) and the Movement for Islamic Reform in Arabia (MIRA).

Nevertheless, as a pressure group in Muslim society, Islamic fundamentalism still flourishes. The United States's war on terrorism and the escalating Israel–Palestine conflict have revived Islamic militancy, especially in the Middle East and central and southern Asia. As long as the United States and the West appear to be pursuing aggressive policies in their relationships with the Arab world, the terrorists of Al Qaeda, Hamas, and Islamic Jihad will find an audience for their message of hate.

This Egyptian version of the popular quiz show, "Who Wants to Be a Millionaire?" demonstrates how the Arab world continues to be influenced by Western culture, despite the efforts of the fundamentalists. In July 2001 the conservative religious authorities issued a fatwa condemning the show as sinful and a form of gambling.

While the terrorist groups try to influence world opinion with suicide bombs and hijackings, there is another, quieter movement going on, influencing Muslim society at a deeper level. Some predict that the future for Islamic fundamentalism will not be about violent change, but about the day-to-day efforts by members of Islamic groups to make Muslim countries more religious. For example, the Muslim Brotherhood is active in Egypt with campaigns to ban alcohol, **pornography,** and TV satellite dishes, and impose stricter dress codes. In Lebanon, Jordan, and Kuwait, fundamentalists wage court battles and press campaigns against "un-Islamic" writers and artists.

"Countries [in the Middle East] with secular governments are more religious than they were even twenty years ago. And so these movements, instead of being revolutionary, are becoming evolutionary, pushing for incremental [gradual] change."

Michael Dunn, editor of the *Middle East Journal,* March 2000.

Fundamentalists in power

There are places in the world where fundamentalism has managed to take center stage, in countries like Iran, Bhutan, and Saudi Arabia. Fundamentalists achieved success in these countries because most of their populations were deeply religious and had little experience of **secularism**. Yet each of these regimes has had difficulties in keeping out Western and **secular** influences. They have remained in power either because they have gradually softened their fundamentalist principles, or—in the case of Bhutan —because they have made themselves a completely closed society.

It is likely that future fundamentalists, if they achieve power, will be faced with this kind of choice. If their people are able to interact with Western democracies, they will encounter greater freedoms for women and **ethnic minorities**, as well as freedom of worship. Some may dislike these freedoms, and be offended by Western liberal attitudes, but others will be attracted to them, and this will always cause problems for fundamentalist regimes.

Bhutanese children doing their school homework. Since Bhutan closed its doors to outside influence, its people have become among the poorest in the world.

"*There is no clash of civilizations between Islam and the West. The really decisive battle is taking place within Muslim civilization, where ultraconservatives compete against moderates and democrats for the soul of the Muslim public.*"

Robert W. Hefner, Department of Anthropology, Boston University, May 2002.

Timeline

1730s–1750s The First Great Awakening

1736 Al-Wahhab begins to preach his message of Islamic revivalism

1745–1800 Wahhabism spreads throughout the Arabian peninsula

1800–1830s The Second Great Awakening

1830s–1840s The start of the American millenarian movement

1859 Publication of Darwin's *The Origin of Species,* which sparked the evolution controversy

1875 Formation of the Islamic Movement

1897 First Zionist conference held in Basel, Switzerland

1902 Founding of the American Bible League to promote the Bible as a work of literal truth

1910–1915 Publication of *The Fundamentals of the Faith* by a group of conservative Protestants

1917 Balfour Declaration: Britain promises support in the establishment of a homeland for Jewish people in Israel

1918 Collapse of the Ottoman Empire

1919 Millenarians change their name to World's Christian Fundamentals Association

1920 The term "fundamentalism" is invented

1922 Harry Emerson Fosdick gives influential sermon, "Shall the Fundamentalists Win?"

1925 Scopes trial

1928 Formation of the Muslim Brotherhood, an Islamic revivalist group, in Egypt

1930s–1940s Period of consolidation for Christian fundamentalism

1938 The Muslim Brotherhood begins to engage in terrorism

1948 The establishment of the state of Israel. 750,000 Palestinian Arabs become refugees.

1950s–1960s Emergence of the Christian Evangelical movement

1960–1966 Sayyid Qutb writes his influential works on the creation of a pure Islamic state

1967 Israel defeats Arab forces in the Six Day War. Israeli territory expands to include the West Bank and Gaza Strip.

1968 The PLO turns to terrorism

1973 Abortion is made legal in the United States

1974 Establishment of the Jewish fundamentalist group Gush Emunim

1975–1988 The era of the Moral Majority and the televangelists

1978 Formation of Hamas, an Islamic fundamentalist terrorist group

1979 A revolution in Iran brings the fundamentalist regime of Ayatollah Khomeini to power

1980 Gush Emunim turns to terrorism

1980s–1990s A period of widespread Islamic militancy and terrorism

1981	Emergence of Sikh fundamentalism
1982	President Sadat of Egypt is assassinated by Islamic fundamentalists
1984	Indian troops attack Sikh Golden Temple in Amritsar, killing many including the fundamentalist Sikh leader, Bhindranwale
1988	Christian fundamentalist Pat Robertson campaigns for the Republican nomination for U.S. president
1988	Upsurge of Hindu fundamentalism
1989	Ayatollah Khomeini issues a *fatwah* against Salman Rushdie
1989	A fundamentalist regime comes to power in Sudan under Hassan al-Turabi and Omar Hassan al-Bashir
1989	The formation of the Christian Coalition
1990	Jewish fundamentalist leader Meir Kahane is assassinated
1992	Hindu fundamentalists destroy ancient Muslim mosque in India
1994	29 Muslims killed by Jewish fundamentalist, Baruch Goldstein
1995	Israel's prime minister assassinated by a Jewish fundamentalist
1995–2001	The Taliban rules Afghanistan
1997	A reformist government is elected in Iran
1998	Osama bin Laden issues his *fatwah* calling for Americans to be killed
1999	The BJP, a Hindu fundamentalist party, takes power in India
2001	Passenger planes are flown into buildings in the United States killing more than 3,000 people. The attacks are organized by the Islamic fundamentalist group, Al Qaeda.
2002	More than 180 people are killed in a bomb blast at a nightclub in Bali, Indonesia. The attack is blamed on local Islamic terrorists with possible links to Al Qaeda.

Resources

Books

Brasher, Brenda. *Encyclopedia of Fundamentalism.* New York: Routledge, 2001.

Connolly, Sean. *What's at Issue: War and Conflict.* Chicago: Heinemann Library, 2002.

Mason, Claire. *21st Century Debates: New Religious Movements.* Chicago: Raintree, 2004.

Woolf, Alex. *21st Century Debates: Terrorism.* Chicago: Raintree, 2004.

Glossary

anti-modern movement system of beliefs that is opposed to the culture, technology. and social changes of modern society

baptism religious ceremony in which the person being baptized is sprinkled with or immersed in water to symbolize purification

Bible sacred book of the Christian religion. The Old Testament of the Bible, or Hebrew Bible, is a sacred book of the Jewish religion.

burka all-over garment with veiled eyeholes, worn by some Muslim women

caliph Muslim ruler or spirtual head

caliphate territory over which a caliph's rule extends, or the time for which it lasts

caste any of the four main hereditary classes into which Hindu society is divided. A person's caste determines his or her social status.

conservative follower of conservatism—a political or religious philosophy based on a desire to keep things as they are and to preserve traditional ways of life and behavior

constitution written document outlining the basic laws or principles by which a country is governed

creation science attempt to provide scientific proof for the account of God's creation of the world as described in the Bible

creed set of religious beliefs

democratic used to describe a system of government where the leaders have been elected freely and equally by all its citizens, or a country with such a system

Democrat member of the Democratic Party, one of the two major political parties of the United States

Dharma teachings of the Buddha

doctrine rule or principle that forms the basis of a religious belief

ethnic minority group in a society whose members precieve themselves, and who are perceived by others, as culturally distinct. Ethnic minorities are often, but not always, the objects of discrimination.

evolution, theory of theory by which all species, including humans, are thought to have developed from earlier forms of life

exploitative refers to policies or practices making unfair use of somebody

gender roles different parts that men and women are expected to play in society

Hadith collection of the sayings of Muhammad, the founder of Islam, and stories about his life. The Hadith is a source of guidance for Muslims.

halakah body of Jewish law, beginning with the first five books of the Hebrew Bible, and developed by rabbis

immigrant person who settles in a country he or she was not born in

Industrial Revolution period beginning in the second half of the 18th century when Britain, Europe, and the United States experienced a surge in productivity and wealth due to the widespread adoption of large-scale, mechanical means of production

jihad struggle for Islam. This can be interpreted either as a holy war or as a spiritual striving.

legislation process of making laws

liberalism belief in freedom of thought, speech, action, and religion, and tolerance toward others

literal exactly following the meaning of an original word or text

lobby to try to influence those people making laws

militant extremely active in support of a cause, often to an extent that causes conflict with other people or institutions

millenarian movement movement that believed in Jesus Christ's Second Coming, a final conflict between good and evil, and the end of the world, based on the biblical book of Revelation

missionary somebody sent on a religious mission to spread the faith or to do social and medical work or both

mosque building in which Muslims worship

nationalism belief in the right of one's people to exist as a nation, or belief in the status of one's nation above all others

natural selection process by which creatures best suited to survival in a particular environment find it easier to find a sexual partner and pass on their characteristics to future generations. This, according to Charles Darwin, is how evolution works.

Ottoman Empire Turkish empire established in the late 13th century in Asia Minor, eventually extending throughout the Middle East. The Ottoman Empire came to an end in 1922.

Pentecostal Christian denomination that emphasizes the workings of the Holy Spirit and interprets the Bible literally

pornography magazines, films, books, or other media that depict sexual behavior with the sole purpose of sexually exciting the viewer, reader, or listener. There is often debate about whether or not materials are pornographic.

Qur'an sacred book of Islamic religion, containing teachings about God, advice for living, and stories

rabbi Jewish religious leader, or scholar qualified to interpret Jewish law

racial integration process of opening a community to all, regardless of racial background

radicalism belief in extreme political, economic, or social change

Ramadan ninth month of the Islamic calendar, during which Muslims fast

revivalist movement movement within a religion to reawaken religious commitment.

salvation in the Christian religion, this means deliverance from sin through the sacrifice of Jesus, or through personal acceptance of Jesus as the savior

secular not connected with religion, religious matters, or God

secularism belief that religion should play no part in political life, and should be not be involved in running public institutions

Talmud collection of ancient Jewish writings that makes up the basis of Jewish religious law

televangelism form of Christian evangelism in which the sermons and services are broadcast on television

Torah first five books of the Hebrew Bible, written on a parchment scroll for use in services in synagogues (Jewish places of worship)

Wahhabism very conservative movement within Islam that rejects any innovation that occurred after the third century of Islam

Zionism worldwide movement that sought to establish a Jewish nation in Palestine. Since 1948, Zionists continue to act in support of Israel

Index

DATE DUE

Printed
in USA

HIGHSMITH #45230